CATHY GALVIN
Ethnology

A LOVE SONG FOR CONNEMARA

BLOODAXE BOOKS

Copyright © Cathy Galvin 2026

ISBN: 978 1 78037 772 8

First published 2026 by
Bloodaxe Books Ltd,
Eastburn,
South Park,
Hexham,
Northumberland NE46 1BS.

www.bloodaxebooks.com
For further information about Bloodaxe titles
please visit our website and join our mailing list
or write to the above address for a catalogue.

LEGAL NOTICE
All rights reserved. No part of this book may be
reproduced, stored in a retrieval system, or
transmitted in any form, or by any means, electronic,
mechanical, photocopying, recording or otherwise,
without prior written permission from Bloodaxe Books Ltd.

Requests to publish work from this book
must be sent to Bloodaxe Books Ltd.

Cathy Galvin has asserted her right under
Section 77 of the Copyright, Designs and Patents Act 1988
to be identified as the author of this work.

Cover design: Neil Astley & Pamela Robertson-Pearce.

Printed in Great Britain by Bell & Bain Limited, 303 Burnfield Road,
Thornliebank, Glasgow G46 7UQ, Scotland, on acid-free paper
sourced from mills with FSC chain of custody certification.

Ní bás ach fás

Not death but growth

For Kate, Bridget and Connor

CONTENTS

9   Introduction
11 Preface: Title Deed

Book One: Specimens

15 Island Road
16 Blunt Needles
17 I Collect
18 Boat People
19 Physiography: 1
20 Dusk
21 Women Come to Find Me
22 Hawk
23 Physiography: 2
24 Snow
25 Na Ceachtanna: Lessons
30 Adúirt mo Mhamó
31 An Ghaeltacht
32 Place Names
33 Starlings
35 From the Kitchen on the Edge
36 Back Tonight to a Deserted House: 1
37 Back Tonight to a Deserted House: 2
38 Back Tonight to a Deserted House: 3
39 Saint's Toolkit
40 Warming the Bones
41 Adúirt mo Mhamó Arís
43 Walls
44 Ethnology

Book Two: Mother

47 Waters Break
48 Rough Translation
51 What They Say to a Child
52 Guy's Hospital, London

53   Straight Lines
54   Source
55   Bríd
56   Caoineadh
58   Swell
59   Credo

Book Three: Love Songs of Connacht

63   Mythology
68   Crow
69   Body of the Boat
70   Anraith
72   Man at Rosroe
73   At the Michael Hartnett Festival
74   Folklore Collector
76   Belly of the House
77   Joe
78   The Singer's Centenary: Carna
80   Coventry Carol
81   Shells
82   Playwrights
83   Cromwellian
84   Turn to the Wall

Book Four: Son

87   Before
88   Samhain
89   After
97   Old Woman

99   NOTES & ACKNOWLEDGEMENTS
111 BIOGRAPHICAL NOTE

Introduction

This book is a love song for the people of south Connemara, Ireland. It is sung into the shell of an island cottage built by my great-grandfather for his family after the Great Famine.

The song started as I lay in bed as a child and heard adults in the next room talking in a language, Irish, I did not understand. Their words were rooted in an oral culture which had a particular resonance for 19th-century anthropologists, ethnologists, folklorists and Anglo-Irish Celtic Revivalists. These elites regarded the people of the western seaboard as either an inferior species of being, or a noble Celtic breed, models for the values of a new, free Ireland. Whatever agendas their lives fulfilled for others, my family remained, long into my childhood, on the margins of Europe, and poor, unless they took their chances and emigrated. This work, nonetheless, owes much to how those elites recorded the lives of my people as well as to the language of my ancestors and my upbringing within an Irish family in England.

Then and now, the boats continue to visit the now uninhabited island of Máisean: I have been rowed there in a currach by my uncle and grandmother, as they guided swimming cattle across from the mainland to graze. I have buried my son's heart there.

There is loss and anger within these poems yet the process of writing them has, I hope, also created a different sound, one that suggests a shift of power as well as a continuation of love for people and place. The island girl, recorded and translated by so many socially privileged men and women, has learned to compose the story of her people in the way she chooses.

Preface: Title Deed

Parts of the lands of Mason Island containing together five acres and three roods, or thereabouts, statute measure, situate in the Barony of Ballynahinch and County Galway. There are appurtenant to the said lands the following rights:

The right of cutting and collecting one fifteenth share of all the seaweed growing or cast upon the foreshore of other parts of the island. Parts of Ardnacross Island containing 29 perches or thereabouts and part of Avery island containing 31 perches or thereabouts. The owner is not to keep livestock of any description in the dwelling house.

The lands above described are subject:– To the amount due on foot of £96, being the amount for which the owner has purchased the said lands from the Trustees of the Congested Districts Board for Ireland.

The purchase money is repayable with interest by an annuity of £3.2.5 for the term of 68 and a half years from the 1st day of November, 1901. By half-yearly instalments one every 1st day of May, and 1st day of November.

Signed Pat (John) Connolly 31st day of March 1902.
(Specimen A: cannot read or write).

Registered 15th day of May 1992.
1. 12th September 1974. The note of equities is cancelled. Titles absolute.
2. 14th October 2023. Signed Catherine Connolly Galvin. Great granddaughter of Pat. Granddaughter of Kate. Daughter of Bridget. Mother and grandmother. (Specimen B: Writer).

BOOK ONE

Specimens

In pursuance of the plan adopted by the Dublin Anthropometric Committee of combining the ordinary work of the Laboratory with local investigation in selected parts of the country, and first tried last year in the Ethnographic Expedition to the Aran Islands... Carna was selected as the centre of operations, as from it the islands of Mweenish and Mason, and the primitive district of Mace Head were most easily accessible...we were only able to obtain measurements of thirty-eight men, who, however, from the fixity of type prevailing in this as in most western districts, were fairly representative specimens.

from reports by Charles R. Browne, anthropologist

Island Road

The gable ends grow darker,
fixed points on the horizon
from Mason to Dog Bay.
In between – expanse of sea, of bog,
smoking shoulders of mountains,
squall and rainbow, rock
jiving with the sky.
The road becomes smaller,
heading into my veins.

Blunt Needles

Inward, rowing in, I come as a thief
to steal your life, like a collector.
Outward, rowing out, your gift to me is scented

>island wool, meadow-salted. You know the depth
>of blunt currach oars, the warping frame's long stretch.
>Inward, rowing in, I come as a thief.

Embers heat an iron pot of indigo, limpets
baked on their backs. Ash singes my sketch.
Outward, rowing out, your gift to me is scented.

>You speak of fishbone stitches, honeycomb and cable,
>how women's fingers pulled dark nights over their needles.
>Inward, rowing in, I come as a thief.

Glass un-breaks from your floor to re-jar rusts and golds.
In the light, a quilt of webs, dried ribbons of weeds.
Outward, rowing out, your gift to me is scented.

>Your designs chevron a scalloped storm-shore,
>collaging threads I touch yet have no skill for.
>Outward, rowing out, your gift to me is scented.
>Inward, rowing in, I come as a thief.

I Collect

Rejection. The thing claimed that does not want to be claimed.
A mirror with no reflection.
A weight of landscape. A lightness of stone.
A hand on the shore still clinging to the net.
A skull, flesh on nose, a strand of hair.
A cormorant drowned.
The last gospel of Christ, spoken to an Irish mercenary who spoke it to me in a language I don't understand.
A rope of narrative, an umbilical cord of love.

Boat People

I saw them arrive,
pulled women to the shore.
I saw the coffins
and the ones who turned away.

I saw the cities, mills, bars –
ironed linen and service left behind.
I heard the oystercatcher,
I heard the key turn in the door.

I was with that woman for a long time –
the one who decided to stay,
set me to work gutting fish,
scrubbed my hands and face.

I was with those men who shrank away,
their accents heavy with return and flight.
She gave me her boat. Said *bring back
what was lost on the tide*.

Physiography: 1

In this sub-district:

(A) Blackbird; Black-backed Gull; Black-headed Gull; Blue Tit; Carrion Crow; Chough; Common Mallard; Common Sandpiper; Cormorant; Curlew; Dunlin; Dunnock; Egret; Gannet; Great Tit; Guillemot; Herring Gull; Heron; House Sparrow; Jackdaw; Kestrel; Lapwing; Magpie; Mute Swan; Oystercatcher; Pied Wagtail; Raven; Redshank; Ringed Plover; Robin; Sedge Warbler; Shag; Shelduck; Snipe; Sanderling; Starling; Tern; Wheatear; Wimble; Wren.

(B) List of Surnames of Families and number of Families of each surname:
Barrett (8); Berry (1); Brennan (1); Burke (8); Carroll (1); Casey (6); Clogherty (13); Conneely (31); Conroy (3); Conway (1); Coyne (4); Curren (8); Devane (3); Donohoe (2); Faherty (1); Feeney (2); Fitzpatrick (2); Flagherty (2); Folan (17); Gannon (2); Geary (11); Geraghty (1); Gorham (14); Greene (19); Henue (1); Hernan (5); Joyce (2); Keane (3); Keaney (6); Deely (2); Kilmartin (4); Kineavy (1); King (4); Lavery (1); Lee (4); Lydon (6); McCormack (4); McDonagh (6); McGlue (1); McGrath (6); McHugh (1); Madden (5); Molloy (1); Mongan (2); Moran (1); Mulkerrin (27); Nee (7); O'Brien (2); O'Donnell (3); O'Malea (1); Reilly (1); Ridge (7); Shaughnessy (1); Ward (3); Walsh (5).

Note: Vulnerable to skin and lung disease. Little evidence of sexual immorality or incest – imbecility appears to be rare.

Dusk

Fire on the horizon
floats until an orange eye
disappears from view burning
all that is hidden beyond wind, storm,
fallen walls.

Do not trust
everything unseen is fixed, certain
as seasons, as fruit sugared and stored.
When the horizon shifts to silhouette, rock
to castle,

seal to woman, hooves to man
and starlings are sleeted in flame, streams flood
story to the mouth. Once the horizon
held wonder. Now it holds me in place, tastes
of salt.

Women Come to Find Me

A small spoil-heap,
a sigh of the *sí*
a staring chestnut face,
gone in flight across stone and gorse,
then one, two, three hares
cross my path on the way to the quay.
My women, come to greet me;
prayers answered from the time of loss
to the time of plenty. Too late
to carry their weight of stones.
On this road I see a distant hill.
As a child, I saw an orange sky
that owned me. I am here to learn,
if they will let me.

---

sí: a 'fairy', magical place.

Hawk

  At the edge of my eye
    flight; nearer, nearer
      the sight of opened wings –
        underbelly of your silence.

    Pink and brown of each feather
      in negative against the light
    of the horizon; a small hawk
caught in the wind.

Not yet in your claws. Blink-laugh,
  scream-call; leaning
    from the seen into whatever
disappears into absence.

Physiography: 2

On this island:

(C)   Bell Heather; Bindweed; Birdsfoot Trefoil; Bistort; Bladder Campion; Bramble; Buttercup; Chickweed; Common Daisy; Common Hawkbit; Common Spotted Orchid; Common Thistle; Common Vetch; Cow Parsley; Dock; Early Purple Orchid; Eyebright; Flag Iris; Fleabane; Forget-me-not; Fuchsia; Gorse; Harebell; Honeysuckle; Kidney Vetch; Knapweed; Lady's Bedstraw; Marsh Pennywort; Meadowsweet; Mouse-ear Chickweed; Nettle; Ox Eye Daisy; Oxlip Great Burdock; Pennyroyal; Pink Centaury; Purple Loosestrife; Ragwort; Red Clover; Rock Saxifrage; Rosebay Willowherb; Rushes; Saxifrage; Scarlet Pimpernel; Sea Bindweed; Sea Holly; Sedge; Self Heal; Silverweed; Sheepsbit Scabious; Small Scabious; Snapdragon; Sorrel; Sow Thistle; Spring Gentian; St John's Wort; Stonecrop; Thrift; Tormentil; White Clover; Yarrow; Yellow Bartsia; Yellow Crucifer; Yellow Rattle.

(D) *The district can thus be said to have really no history… and I can find no record of any influx of people from other districts to alter the old strain, and indeed there would be little to tempt them to such a barren district.*

Snow

Although
        a sign marked the place of battle
        there was nothing to warn against
        drinking water from the frozen pool,
        against digging the lily out
        by its roots, biting into the bulb,
        tasting the bitterness of iron; putting
        an ear to the cold earth to hear the beat
        of one word to take back, the horse drum
        on *droim*. We knew the dangers
        of this westward journey, where
        you exposed film under the snow
        to photograph what lies beneath, and I –
        smaller, uncertain – smeared mud
        on my mouth like iced cake, like a child
        on her first birthday, who does not yet
        know the taste and shape of words.
        We had to feel this place in our hands,
        between our teeth   and when we left
        the dark central plain, the treeless hills,
        the buzzard, the waters' crack, I took
        more than a beat – a grain under
        my tongue; whispers, particles
        of woman, cloth, cries, metal
        seeping into bone. It had begun to snow,
        falling on every part of the dark pool,
        falling on the torn root, the crooked
        stone. What is buried absorbs shades of light,
        licks of flickering, fertile, falling phrase:
        the taste of something less proper, new –
        something   unfinished.

---

droim: ridge.

Na Ceachtanna: Lessons

A – *An Bord:* the Table

I hear the phrase *Mamó*
  ag an mbord and the softness
    of the sounds

      takes me to where she is
      at the table, potatoes peeled,
      skins falling to the floor.

          Spears a hot spud with her fork
          for my plate. Nails black
          with muck. When she

                turns to go, the sea and fields
                walk with her through the door.

B – *An Madra:* the Dog

Waiting for them here –

at her side when she comes out gathering
herself into the slow walk to the chicken house,

to the bucket sunk deep for water to pour
into his bowl, a hand steadying him at the neck.

Racing across stony fields he would meet her
at the well, framed by dolls, candles, beads,

children's hair, offerings to a veiled blue-white statue
on the sandy road from *Roisín*, where this madra disappears

> – into my thirst.

C – *An Éan:* the Bird

I smell
        the wings of a bird
as it rests in my hands,
feel the fastness of its heart
feathering the first thimbleful of blood
onto my fingers – its scent still with me,
this *éan*
            beating.

D – *An Cáca Milis:* the Cake

Too sweet this Ireland
sold for branding. Dara Ó Briain
on the telly the desperate face of it,
yapping with the mockneying
Jonathan Ross. Give me the power
to put beauty on the page, to deck
the man or woman who diminishes.
Give me the power to bake
a bitter mongrel cake.

E – *Tá Ocras Orm:* I Am Hungry

Go to Gorham's shop
and say *kay hee will too,*
ask her for *awrawn.*
you said.

Fifty years on,
the shop has gone and though I can spell
cén chaoi a bhfuil tú agus arán,
I can taste none of it.

The first stanza recalls the phonetic pronunciation of *cén chaoi a bhfuil tú?* (how are you?) and *arán* (bread).

Adúirt mo Mhamó

colder than a body
  the sea is waiting
rising in the depths
  of the self
turning traces, dreams
  signs
 in and out
  of the belly
blowing rain back
  to the clouds
melting flesh of sailor
  and child
a whisper at the mouths
  of rivers
the culvert creep
 to odyssey
  in an atom
writing wasteland
  lines of *beannachtaí*
and baptism
 to keep us for a while
  from the other side
if we believe
  we can swim
we will drown

Adúirt mo Mhamó: My grandmother said.

An Ghaeltacht

Paul – Pól – bought himself a boat
and a house. Took land on the island,
drove through mountains on a motorbike.
But these people with the same name as him,
the same DNA, drinking in the same bar,
kept themselves to themselves.
Gave him no work. And in Galway –
well, you might as well be back in Croydon, he said.
All those East Europeans, no one speaking English.
He keeps his curtains drawn, gate padlocked.
I'm told he's packing his bags. Taking
his estuary English over to Durham
where houses are also cheap. In time, it's possible,
they tell me, he might even pick up the language.

Place Names

When I enter the stormy peninsula
of *Iorras Aithneach* through murk, spike and needle

my eye is fixed on the harbour at Cashel
yet soon lost in a world of woven islands.

Safest to drop sail three times
to honour the holy man MacDara,

pay homage to his god and to wonder
at the field of deer on *Cruach na Caoile*.

I won't go to the lands of the east
where Tadhg na Buile caught Spanish

sailors like fish and sold them to the English.
I row ashore at *Máisean*; touch the altar stone.

Starlings

They watched the crash and pull
    of bodies rapturing the waves,
        being raised. Spume
    clapping light; a winter of surprised narcissi.

Abandoned turf-trenches wounding the eye.
        Criss-crossing forgotten roads, cottages once impossible
            to sell; now the booleys of the wealthy –
        the fine, the rucksacked, the Hunter-booted.

To the east, starlings hitchcocked the passing car
    in flight along wall, blow-cropping grass,
        sinking to the glass of bog at twilight. Winged deep
in wet of earth, hidden from the hoofed solidity of horses.

Flat horizon, rock, strangeness of fir, eye of lake.
A wind to be loosed, woven, shout-ridden to the fall.

For food: the cake of bread baked with flour which must be brought from the mainland; fish, which was dried and salted against bad weather. Limpets – turned on their backs and cooked in their shells on the edge of the turf fire – and other crustaceans and potatoes – cooked, in their skins and boiled in seawater. And then the edible sea weeds – dilsk and carrageen moss. They lived on the meagre returns for fish, lobsters, kelp and perhaps wool or knitting. One can believe that the intricate designs in Aran knitting were developed to keep the women's minds away from the perils the men were facing at sea and also to pass the time through the long winters. The knitting is based on traditional stitches – the blackberry stitch, Irish moss stitch, the lobster claw, the fishbone, the honeycomb, the diamond and the cable – all done entirely 'out of their heads' and the garments must not be washed too often to preserve the oiliness in the wool. On island homes, there was often a pot of Indigo simmering in the fire ready to stain the wool for making tweed.

In Mem. Enid Hooper

From the Kitchen on the Edge

Does the sea hurt? I turned away from the strand
to fences, barbed wire, plastic, two old baths, concrete, granite;

turned back inside but you can't stop the tide,
the ker ker ker per-pipetting bird, or throat of lark,

green on black of rock, ribbons of precise light,
open-chested to me, to the sea, to Fraochoileán.

The quay: car with a gaping boot, boats stowed
in metal sheds, cleared for the swift, the gull,

the greening bramble, primrose. Can't turn away
from the smoke-broke women. Cáit had seven children,

some of them do not speak, most are in the ground.
Who spoke: the mountain? The waves? I hear,

do not meddle with what you do not understand.
The sea is eating the window. Who swept the floor,

lit the turf? Piss in a pot beneath the bed,
who emptied it into dung, into straw? Pails of spotted milk,

a table floured with bread. Does the sea hurt?
The sand? Those hands?

Back Tonight to a Deserted House: 1

I look at the page

if even those with the language, the story and the song

say, *now it is gone*

what can there be left for me to sing?

I say – *Dia dhuit*

I say – *how can I find a builder?*

I say – *how can I learn the songs?*

I say – *who can make my boat?*

I say – *the days are long*

filled with the light of birds.

Back Tonight to a Deserted House: 2

Féachaim ar an leathanach

fiú iad siúd leis an teanga, na scéalta agus na hamhráin

dier siad, *anois tá sin imithe*

cad atá fágtha dom le canadh?

Deirim – *Dia dhuit*

Deirim – *cá háit is féidir liom tógálaí a aimsiú?*

Deirim – *cé a thógfaidh mo bhád?*

Deirim – *go bhfuil na laethanta fada*

lán de sholas agus ceiliúradh na n-éan.

Back Tonight to a Deserted House: 3

When you hear the song of strangers
from the ground floor of your house
and on investigation find
no one there – and move,
from room to room, while they call from the roof,
you must decide whether to join them
in celebrating the impossibility of the night sky.

Saint's Toolkit

What does a saint need for a journey to an island?
Boat. Tools. Cloak. Bible. Water and food. Sky. Moon.
Sun. Stars. Birds. Astrolabe. Her closest servants. Song.
When she gets there: a laptop. Planning permission.

Warming the Bones

I have dug up the bones,
smoothed them, painted them white,
arranged them around the empty hearth to keep warm.
The souls at the door
dressed in flannels and shawls
look at each other, unsure
who has called them up
from their boat in the harbour.

They whisper, one passes me a cloak.
The one who gave birth to my mother
stands, gives me her hand.

Adúirt mo Mhamó arís

When I was a child, the men came – the English doctor, and policemen. They demanded the men of the island gather together to be photographed, their heads and limbs measured. Our men feared the doctor was measuring them for uniforms, that they would be forcibly conscripted to fight for King and country in some nameless war. Since there is always some use for what washes up on the shore, we made the doctor welcome. In our home, he wrote of our 'fragile prosperity' from working the land and sea – from fishing (lobster, herring, mackerel, bream) and trading in kelp. He wrote: *The introduction of the National School has resulted in a measure of literacy amongst the youngest children, a confidence in speaking and writing the English language, that will inevitably reduce the population further as they leave this existence behind to improve their prospects beyond Connemara. There is little to lament in this since the island and neighbouring districts have no civilisation and no written account of their history.*

His language was so distant, his fears were so apparent, his beliefs brutal. He remembered me and later wrote: *I have spent a charming afternoon in the company of a young child called Katie, who was sent to me by her mother with tea in a cup and saucer as I rested at the crossroads. Such grace has not been commonly in evidence on my travels. She enquired as to what I had studied in order to qualify for this exercise in observing her people. It seemed her curiosity was keen, her knowledge limited, a state of affairs her questioning suggested she also detected in my manner. My abilities, she told me, made me entirely unsuited to island life since I have no Irish, do not know how to handle or mend a boat, how to fish or to burn kelp. She said it was clear that, unlike her father, I did not know how to make or mend nets or shoes, build or thatch a house, make a cradle or a coffin.*

Our conversation later awakened questions: where does the undeniable knowledge of record and measurement serve us well in science and ethnography? How does the impossibility of measuring the inner passions and the inherited social memory of a people hinder our greater understanding?

Oh, how I loved to tease him.

Walls

There's no anvil, brooch, harrow-pin.
The currach's broken, walls stand without a roof.
All that's left: a bureau containing bills,
cards, scarves, a Will.

You're not in view but I can hear a breath
– the well-made dress and phrase.
My made things broke long ago.
They had little purchase on this world.
The creed, letters I do not read.
Solid seem the things that slip away.
Leaving us bone.

We stake a claim, lay foundations,
build and watch it fall.
Within, the comforts that ease survival.
We cut back wilderness, tame, contain
sycamore, birch, bramble, willow, grass.
All return.

Our walls come down, consolations go.
We do not come back. Take away it all
and what is left is who we are.
Our homes are built to go.

Ethnology

Smelling of earth and ethanol,
the scholar with soft leather gloves
lifted my head from a box
lined with velvet, unpacked
my skull on a polished desk,

took the measure of me,
this other species,
when are bones no longer our own?
Could not bring himself to touch
the shreds of flesh on my nose.

I had waited for the moon
to rise over rocks
where I searched for seals, their singing
making me pause
                              at Trinity
wait for letters written to the Provost
that may yet bring me home
to turf, stones, lines of tourists.

When there was flesh
on my childhood I walked
the cow road to the cliff edge,
lifted blue eggs where they rested
on the ground, warm in my hands.
Placed them in a box
as treasure. Knowing they were where they would not crack

into flight.

BOOK TWO

Mother

When a number of blackened boards and pieces of bone had been thrown up with the clay, a skull was lifted out, and placed upon a gravestone. Immediately... the old woman took it up in her hands and carried it away by herself. Then she sat down and put it in her lap – it was the skull of her mother – and began keening over it with the wildest lamentations.

J.M. Synge, *The Aran Islands*

Waters Break

                    Stroke my brow in the cot.
        In your shawl of pitch and ice, unmake an ocean bed,
throw boulders at the wide-eyed, headless cabins,
flare fingers
           of phosphorus into the drumroll of the hurricane.

          You are alone in a tower wreathed in cigarette smoke
                where the city washes below:
I am away, getting it wrong,
not hearing the doctors' footsteps, not seeing what they cut from you
      and throw to the pail.

      Swimming in rain within the murmurs of *Marias*, of *a ghrá mo chroí*,
            you storm. Not a song – the wind's roar.
                  Not a song – an ecstasy. Not a song –
    a birth moan broken over my feet. Fish, in a bucket,
left by the door. Shoals of breathing silver
    abandoned by the tide.

              Put on the island as a dress, and when you wake,
    put on a coat of fathoms. What does the water want?
           O…the O…
        the O of a child's face crowning,
    the eye of the moon. The opening …
        opening…O…
breaking on the shore.

Marias: Hail Mary prayers; *a ghrá mo chroí*: familiar endearment meaning my love.

Rough Translation

I

Here is a boat.

   My mother dreams this boat. She looks over the bow. There is no crew. She cannot reach land. She is on a dark sea, pulling away from the island. Light falls over her walnut dressing table, silver brushes laid out on lace. She stands, bends to the mirror, running crème through her short brown hair to tame the curl. Adjusts a brooch. The room smells of eau-de-cologne and the street outside. I like to taste her flaking lipstick on my fingers. I like to watch her secretly, observing how she twists back to adjust a stocking and how she bends to slip a foot into her heels. Her soft eiderdown is the void my life floats on. The sound of a ticking bedside clock, of the throaty blackbird who builds her nest outside the window. Settling between sleep and wakefulness, there are footsteps on a warm pavement. I pull the boat back and hold it in my hands. Blue paint and black tar. I lift it from the waves. My mother is safe.

   She has not yet been swept away.

II

Child. Listen. Once, I rowed you towards the island. I pulled the boat up onto the beach. You took my hand as we made our way along a track towards the crossroads. Where the path rises up from the harbour, we looked down over slabs of granite, across fields to mountains. We saw grasses dotted with wild flowers and the hidden eggs of seabirds, a shallow lake, a seashore of oystercatchers.

> *Are there ghosts on the island?* you asked.
> I said: *You go your way. And they go theirs.*

You will never speak my words for earth, sea or wind and I can no longer taste them. Your song won't hold my tune, only theirs. My dreams are in English. Words for something better than a tongue dipped in salt and earth. They will want you to succeed but never more than them.

> *put your shoulders back*

Between your finger and your thumb, there's no skill for knitting. My needles, in your right hand, have been digging me out of the grave for fifty years. The squat pen rests in your left. When you use these tools, are you a traitor, a fraud or a fool?

> *stop skulking behind*

I thought of you today, the way our narrow bones begin to flex and crack with all that time drags to the floor. The pull of bags, children, body. The ball bearing down on neck, spine.

> *like an orphan.*

III

Mother –
I cannot do this lightly – say
your skull is in my handbag I have dug it from the ground.
Carried it for many years.
All clever-clever. Though you might prefer that to this:
why did you leave me?

What They Say to a Child

Put your shoulders back.   She was so beautiful.
Stop walking like a navvy.   She was very – nervy.
Speak up for yourself.   If she is going to die, why doesn't she die soon?
Get out and play.   Go on, have a Babycham.
Don't be so timid.   Get yourself an education, then you can clean toilets.
Stop slouching   She didn't want you to wear glasses and not be pretty.
Stop biting your nails.   She would never have stayed married to your father.
Skulking behind like an orphan.   She was the peacemaker.
Get your face out of the book.   Your mother was a saint.
Go and stick up for yourself   Your mother would be ashamed of you.
Put your shoulders back.   You remind me of her, the smile, the way you move.

Guy's Hospital, London

Once a river flowed
under the pavings of our street
to where suburban floodplains
waterfall to the sea. A tower.
Thirty-four floors. On the twenty-second
you contain all in a single room. A photo. Rosary beads.
Windows open to the city. A lift brings me up
to you. A butterfly flies in. You set it free.
It comes again. You remember the raven
on a roof, the white bull in a field,
the heron on a rock. Seaweed.
A clock stopped at midnight.

Straight Lines

straight lines cut
to the granite of a Connemara
wall, brambles salt-burned.

I'm suspended

this home is not where the light
once lay on the eyelids of sleeping children
or where grandchildren play.

I do not create the consolation of a continuity,

do not have a trustworthy history.
The white-blue mottled sky of winter
light changes everything.

In the mirror, the face that age has sculpted
to make your face. I taste you,
with a tongue that can't twist sound

to mimic an ancient or contemporary world
but finds a way towards the warmth of blood
flowing to pump around your heart,

your womb ready, already filled with what
I am become in your absence, a child giving birth
to a mother, a toucher of skin through the cracks of walls,

a ghost, waiting for the ground.

Source

the well no longer fills
outside does not come in
there is a keening in the knowledge
that it will not fill again
when the tap no longer turns
and the river has run dry
when the breast no longer floods
there is a keening in the knowledge
that it will not fill again

Bríd

In the boat we held hands
where the oarsman could not see,
not saying this would be your last visit.
Your carved face at the prow.
Your tears, lost in salt,
carrying me in.

Caoineadh

Here where the stones shield the dark harbour

I wait now alone, stand by the ocean

The wind at my back, her emptiness calling

The blackness beyond, rows your dreaming home

Rows your dreaming home, my love, *a ghrá mo chroí*

I stroke your hair back, I weep and I kiss you

Your head in my lap, I rub your hands warm

Slip gold on your finger, the ring they took from you

The ring they gave to me, lift you in my arms

To the anger inside me, for all that was taken

I stand on the granite, a flawed empty vessel

I pull you towards me , I shelter your body

I was inside you, I want you inside me

Bríd Ní Chonghaile, why did you leave me?

O my love, *a ghrá mo chroí*, it's time to come with me

A fire is waiting, a home ready for you

See by the window, a bowl of wild flowers

A child picked this morning. I hold your small hands

Touch our ring on your finger. I look in your eyes

I hold you and hold you. No match for what killed you

Please stay here with me, though you may not want to

Though you may not want to, my love, *a ghrá mo chroí*

I praise you and thank you, for a child's slow beginning

A foot on the land, a foot in the water

I will make your bed ready, with pillows of feathers

Cook lamb in the embers, warm milk for the coffee

Open the window, the cry of the curlew

Your daughter to serve you, to lay you in balm.

Lay down in balm, my love, *a ghrá mo chroí*

I see a mother who loses her children

Row your wounding to me, my love, *a ghrá mo chroí*

I will carry you home, open the window

To the cry of the curlew, to the place of the dark stones

Stand at the ocean, hear your desire singing

The brightness beyond, rows your body home

Swell

In the bath, water
slicks her skin.
A child who lies
perfect, knowing
what she sees is
not allowed, her
body changing,
gaining power.

In the bed, weaving
under the sheets
as they touch her
bare skin and she is older –
her mother wanders in
and smiles, her child
lost in pleasure.

We are seals, she and I.
Beneath and above
the swell of birth.

Credo

I believed she and I did not have a story.
I believed she and I did not matter.
I believed there had never been an us.
I believed she had been forgotten.
I believed it was best to forget.
I began to read the stories of other people
                                      people much more important than us.

BOOK THREE
Love Songs of Connacht

The multitude of characteristic idioms and of those charmingly expressive turns of speech which one meets with daily among the peasantry is so great as to make the work a perfect treasure-house of rich jewels of thought... Dr Hyde deserves well, not only of his country, but of all scientific investigators and philologists.

Freeman's Journal, 1893

Mythology

1 *When I, Dr Hyde, Went West*

She spoke and sang to me the Love Songs of Connacht. There were often verses missing, or variations on many verses of poetry I had found in Roscommon. But it was what she didn't say that haunted me; the way she had of looking directly into my eyes. I will not judge her. The women offer a melody and passion in their songs which is frequently disquieting. The knowledge of the Bards, of learned men, has long gone. We are left with the fragments of poetry the peasants scraping a living along the westerly Atlantic seaboard can remember; we are left with what they may choose to tell us.

2 *Choosing What to Say to Dr Hyde*

I will tell him about fire, lying black as burned coal,
And he will say, *no not black like that, black as sloe.*
Tell of being held high to pick blossom from the furthest tree,
 Black soles on a whitened floor, the way one boy could dance me.

I will say his laugh was a note that dropped splintering into ice,
A spread-webbed, white-blue, black-bruising.
Over peat crushed by boots on a cottage floor,
Like the morning of my forced wedding.

I will tell him my story, this stranger, this old man,
This song-collector. I will tell him and he will never know
How I burned for one boy's beauty, how the river flowed
And roared at his coming, at the fury of his kissing.

And this man will write: *love is the colour of blackberries,*
And the colour of a raspberry on a fine sunny day.
Not that my tongue still tastes him, now he has gone.
To the west this old man should not have come.

The stone is sharp. The lichen cold.

3 *Choosing What to Say to My Love*

Your muscled body flows like water
And the wind catches your hair.
I have watched, and waited
For you to find me, for you to care;
Wondered why you didn't dare
Take all we had made together,
All you had shown me,
Your kiss, your hand,
There. Your kiss, your hand, there.
Your kiss, your hand, there.

4 *What Women Never Say*

They fall. Stone walls down.
What is there to contain?
Rains come down, drown
these papers. Certifying,
claiming the dead, wed, born.

Bog feed.

We must be unnamed.
The same names.
First and surnames. Owned
back to where we
looked from the mountains
across the land of Mweenish
and Mason. Stepped in to
the ocean. Shed shawls,
shape. Fed on fish,
bodied for the *uisce*.

Our men in currachs oared
the cold babies. Lulled
by sea and *sí*. Sang
them to sleep. Buried
their ghosts. Infants
never named.

They lie with and to us.
We carry their names,
heavy, for them. Unweighted
in the green of foam and twilight;
in our cries, the rock of starlight,
they hold our changing forms.
afraid. The known unknown.

I will un-name those names now,
for my grandmother,
who I was named for.
Shed the names of husbands.
For her before her before
her before her before
her before.

Fire food.

Crow

We sip soup
at the oak table with a view from the window
where the poet watched his Crow.
It suited him well, the stark proportions of a house
built for the seaweed agent.
So much profit in a tonne of back-break, sold for saltpetre, exploding
in gunpowder.

Body of the Boat

My cousin Tómas has her
        in his yard
ribs open to feral cats and his boat-builders cut.

Sex and Lost, nicknames for those English boys,
                once provided
her with white sails: mainsail, foresail and jib.

They took her to Boffin. Put the *Ave Maria*
        on the literary map:
                Pat –

bring the Ave-Maria round to Glassillaun.
        Told her story
in the Pier Bar where customers signed the Visitors Book.

Her fame drew Charles Monteith, the big man.
                from Faber;
journalists on freebies from Dublin, Scandinavia.

Watching his friend, Lost could not admit
        losing control,
tiller thrust against his thigh: fish-hooked.

While Sex held a young woman's hand on deck,
                he remembered
cruising the cloister, succursal seed, his wife and child.

Remembered he was not a sailor
        he was – what –
a tug; the outboard's spark, falling in a pit-cage of waves.

Anraith

(for Tim Robinson)

Collect it when you return for tea,
he said. My forgotten umbrella
left in the corner of his hall.
The chronicler of Connemara
always kept things safe: memories
in three volumes; knew the place
where a ruin is all that remains
of Miss Moore of Antrim's dream,
to save the forgotten people
from famine and from Rome
with bowls of soup and a church,
a school, in the field by the sea.

He had walked with friends
to find what he called *traces
of grace* in salt-meadows where
her buildings are long gone –
the carved limestone tomb
of Archibald T. Hamilton
all that could be found in the field.
Those soup-kitchen saviours
of souls were themselves starved,
their suppliers on the long road
turned back, their boat sunk.
The horse of the man
who helped them, drowned.

My chronicled ancestors
spoke of their revenge –
a donkey tethered to the church
bell so that it rang all night;
songs of rebellion sung
yet nothing said of a holy
building gutted by fire where,
later, they removed every stone.

He wrote how the Clifden pastor
would sail to the strand
to preach; a small band
gathered to hear Miss Betts
of Knockboy play her harmonium,
whatever the weather. In the rain
he would shelter her in his certainties,
in the Lord, under his stout umbrella.

Anraith: soup

Man at Rosroe

The stranger takes his dinner,
weighs blue-silver in his hands,
pays with pennies.

On his fingers, mackerel tang,
ink of sunset in water,
flakes of fjord.

In the house, light of thought on paper,
of oil lamp, remembered:
battlefield flowers, small-boy days.

On a knife, pink flesh slowly
peeled and sliced, an iron pan.
Space time and deity

the only worthy questions. His brother
playing Brahms, saying
Take your scepticism away. It's seeping under the door.

He considers that the verbs –
believe, wish and want – have the grammatical form
possessed by cut, chew and run.

On the quay, belly full,
papers burned, eyes raised,
he watches for birds. For boats.

At the Michael Hartnett Festival

No one spoke well of him
when he was alive, a drinker
says in the pub.

Aisling puts down
her pint, takes the speaker
by surprise, says:

the man I loved,
though he was hard to love,
was born

troubled by two tongues
and second sight; he turned
my words to politics

where they died
but his words are alive

are sadness sunk
to the bottom
of the lake

are anger in the crack
of ligaments, blood
on stone.

He was what a man
becomes when composed
by birds.

Folklore Collector

There was poetry in every house, she said.
You can't separate poetry from the land,
it doesn't have roots. A tongue unanchored
to a singing throat, a song no longer sacred,
or understood.

                    Once we stood in a field.
What have you read? she asked. *Bit of Hobbes,
Hegel, Marx: Ricoeur. Nothing really.*

                  Wind blew clouds away
to where we sit today: hearing verses
in the sound of spades un-slicing; reeds
un-feathering from a roof. Praying for music
from children who never learned to make

a boat, a cradle or a coffin.

She knows the weight of the work done,
recording equipment carted down rutted lanes
in the wet to storytellers, to those seeking fame,
or sporting a poor-mouth wisdom that rarely fools.

Yet when, in the *óstán*, she orders
tea, in Irish, she did not expect the young girl
to answer her in English.

　　　　　　　　All those *sean-nós* sacredly
taped, all the time it took, and where's it all heading?
There's no one left to talk to; others don't speak.
And the young waitress? Being cool has a lot to answer for.

óstán: hotel; *sean-nós* ('old style'): unaccompanied singing in Irish.

Belly of the House

Crossing your threshold, time after time,
I believed your buried mouth,
its falling walls and gaping hearth, had lost its tongue.

That your soft language was too hard to learn,
though a little application proved me wrong,
crossing your threshold, time after time.

Through the door I saw abandoned ships,
a blackbird in the ash, a spinning-wheel unspun.
I believed your buried mouth

had been opened by the enemy, in not-so-secret ways,
to force-feed you silence, hunger and isolation,
crossing your threshold, time after time.

That you had sent me back to them, in the belly of a horse,
to surprise them at their game, learn their imperial ways.
I believed your buried mouth; I speak with foreign words.

From the belly of the house, feel a breath
of singing in the eyes of empty windows.

Joe

The song collector stayed in Glinsc with Colm Ó Caodháin
and from Treasa heard 'The Herding of Calves' – '*Seoladh na nGamhna*' –
and spoke of the Aran man he saw dance in his rubber shoes.
Was up for the nights at The Zetland, talking until dawn,
the parties in every house. There are advantages to an isolated place.
He was told my grandfather Joe Mac Conaola in *Roisín na Mainiach*
would give him a sea shanty, was told to come at noon.
Walking up the path, he learned Joe wasn't there.
They say what happens in a good song lives somewhere in the gaps.

The Singer's Centenary: Carna

Song finds a road to his throat, to the film,
to the recording and back to us
    He cannot help being the pure voice of it.

on plastic chairs in the hall. As we look at the screen,
    I remember the rough tapes he made for her on a Philips machine
we can see his bone-tired features, hear the ancient nerve,

    sweeter than a pipe, and for the purpose of wooing
knowing in the pub he'd catch the laugh, the loss, the stamping foot
with the neck of a bottle in his mouth whenever he wasn't singing.

of the spalpeen, far, far from home.
    I didn't know he had a wife
A voice velvet with the breath,

    and children he deserted.
the space of stone; down, down, down
    I can hardly remember being sober at the time.

to where the bonds of words don't need to be dressed in fine clothes,
    I heard accounts of his death, a eulogy by the Bishop of Galway.
where you trust each part of you

    My ex always said they never made love
is enough to stand and sing
    and though of course I refused to believe her,

lyrics with the harp of water, whistle of bird,
    the memories
and hidden rebellion, a sea of wrecks

make me wonder if she was telling
in Bradford, Glasgow, Chicago, in an archive, in a bottle.
the truth after all.

Coventry Carol

You did not sing in Irish or in English.
Never told me what the English did to your people,
were clear you did not want an Irish husband,
someone who might sing sweetly and leave his wife behind,
become a father like yours who did not feed his own children.
When the Irish began bombing Birmingham,
and a shopkeeper refused to serve me in my Catholic
school uniform, your silence filled my mouth.

Shells

                                                          I remember her foot
                                                     in the palm of my hand.

Lifting skulls from the sand
of Máisean. Stroking their bones.
Don't be afraid. Hold their knuckles.

Carry shells in your pocket.
Pick shells from the strand.

An empty mouth
A silenced tongue
Hold her fingers
Lift her up.

Larks resting in the ground where waves pinkle stones.
The only word for water, ishker, *uisce,* ishker –
sand stroked by the salty ishk. Pollen and turf
sit heavy on the lungs. I breathe deep.
There is only this.

                                                           I remember her foot
                                                     in the palm of my hand.

Playwrights

Scene One

The kitchen of a rural cottage in the West of Ireland. The room contains three rocking chairs, a table and an old electric oven. A single electric lightbulb hangs from the low ceiling. In the chairs sit three men, MARTIN, BRIAN *and* JOHN.

MARTIN: What the fuck are you doing here?

JOHN: Some dreams I have had in this cottage seem to give strength to the opinion that there is a psychic memory attached to certain neighbourhoods.

BRIAN: And it was the goddess's aim and cherished hope that here should be the capital of all nations.

MARTIN: Piss off home the lot of ye.

Blackout

Cromwellian

Kill the King, he says. I am standing on the quay
built centuries before by one of Cromwell's men.

Then: *They had a garrison at Aran. Some stayed
and married. I'm one of them.* He smiles, stirring

the pot with a bayonet dipped in royal blood.
I believe in the people. And not in God.

Turn to the Wall

and sing

of lighthouse beams
that fall on black waves

cigarettes smoked
at the back of mills

thin blue paper and biro:
saying a novena for ye

boats pulled to shore
bigger boats pushed to

a better life.

There are no children
here. Just crack

of jackdaw. Maybe
they were right

to leave an island
the mainland in sight

Turn to the wall
& sing of all

we pay for. Hear how
they want us to let them go.

BOOK FOUR

Son

> Water has no character just thirst.
> I wait for salt to heal as the sea hollows out the emptiness.
> Hear the water spill my voice.

Before

One day your call
comes and we say
little.

What is there to say?
Cord tight around your neck.
Hanging between death
and life from that moment.

Belt of Orion
pinned in your eye.
My son, gone to the Bens,
miscalculating all.

Born, already torn
from acceptability,
between my legs. Blue,
a doctor and nurse
silent.

There was a childhood,
forcing Lazarus
through normality.

Am I your mother,
bringing life at
your first
stone breath –
disintegration?

Samhain

        Cailleach stands
        on one foot
        one eye closed
        to watch her sea-god
        betrayer *Manannán*
        who took her skin

        as a bag to carry
        his treasure –
        the memory
        of speech –
        while she carries
        souls between worlds

at night

the butterfly scratches with her fingers until
I feel your hand on my shoulder, turn on the light,
eye-flash of quartz diorite, yellow ragwort.
I ask, do we only love what we can touch?
You say: the wind, the bell, the breath, the cry,
the footstep.
                You say: trust me.

After

I

                                                           down in the bowels of Hades
                                     am given your heart in a wooden box.
                         Leave holding you against me like a baby –
                             wrapped in a bag in the boot of my car.
              Travel through the Black Mountains, take you on a ferry
       to the shadow of the Bens. Place you on the boards of a currach.

    In my dreams I never arrive.

Silver band of light on a grey horizon.
What escaped when they opened
the door of your body?
What stayed in your shroud?
All I didn't do.

I carried you. I must dig this ground.
Because the time is of sparrows,
the crackle of weed without tide,
a shrimp's dart, a low heat,
bees. Buried thunder.

Because the sky breaks
and falls through the white light
of a fly's delicate wings:
see its blood where my wrist
touched it. Now there is a distant plane –

then linnets. All that lies within
the language I cannot speak.
There is new life. There is growing old.
Tell me, if you know, how to live,
to love, to return.

Looking at the three towers,
two gable ends, one chimney.
Can't keep anything or anyone with me.
I'm no steward to this place.
Ships move beyond.

Son of man, flesh of woman,
along the path – dandelion, thistle,
scabious, buttercup, daisy –
to the stones in the field of the house.
Down through the past,

through sand, peat and subsoil,
to lay your heart in holy water,
a covering of lichened stones from walls built
by men, our men, we never met.
Their ruin open as your chest.

Impotent in this language –
can't find the voice of a child,
all the *fadas* wrong, the tenses wrong,
can't remember numbers, the months of the year.
The policeman came to the door

and I knew because I knew when
you wouldn't hold me, as your face
held still and melted,
please sit down –
it would be better if you sat down.

You come to me in a dream,
laughing, saying *look at my hands!*
Your bitten nails healed.
The day you died I held you on the stairs
as you passed through me.

Do you want a cup of tea? Go
away. Come in. Hold me.
In the wash, speckled stones shot with iron quartz,
in the down-tread and up-birth
of geology,

I crush your heart
to my belly, willing every atom
back into my body
where bone, hair, flesh,
can be remade – you safe,
never born.

A gold corner of granite
pressed between my breasts
where I think of your heart,
how I can keep it warm,
against a slate sea and the shades of *Cloch na Rón*.

II

In a cottage where the Sacred Heart and Instagram converge,
this one is being tortured as burning oil is poured over her head
by her spinster daughter. This one is offering her mouth, as a joke,
to the flies of the priest and isn't Martin slamming the bastarding

old ghosts of Connemara with a hammer, a skittering line of despair.
In a cottage where Ikea prints and the view over the bay converge,
Dublin 4 settles in for scallops and sauterne to lament
the lack of builders but plan the next step with the confidence that
   staycations

are worth the investment. In a cottage where my great uncle falls
dead on the eve of his wedding, I take a stone from my son and place it
in the walls where a wooden beam may once have held a floor.
His inheritance – this ruin open to the sky – converges with a heart

too big for a long life. The sea rises. I wanted to rebuild but like your man
says, where can you find a builder? And if I did… why can't I let go?
Wonder am I now McDonagh's ghoulish old whore or is there something
beyond the caricature? Something more?

III

I became a mountain
young. I feel where the sun
flies along the valley casting shapes
then is gone – rivers, streams,
clitter, rushing bone-scored glaciers.

Deeper than denial.
Sometimes I sense the trees behind me,
breathing. A child let go of a mother,
a mother let go of a child.
This is not a magical incantation.

But what if he were not of this world,
the red-haired man in the graveyard
at Omey, the small man, who disappeared.
And what if all the birds we have seen – heron,
robin, curlew – were really omens in flight?

And what if these seas,
under rich copper and gold
layerings of light, furling
islands of aesthetes, speak of
all we will one day understand?

Wrapped in a cloak of calico,
you are with the men of the sea,
sure of your place. The kestrel took
the young blackbird. I want mercy,
not sacrifice.

Small loaves of rock in my hands,
thrown to the strand from the Laurentia-Dalradian
with marble, quartzite, granite, limestone, *cloch bhreac*,
carried back to the rest of your body, the London clay settling.
The rest of you lies near a dustbin, near a path,

near the homeless who sit near you
smoking crack in the litter-blown cemetery.
I lay these sanded sea-washed loaves above.
You, a warrior, beneath.
Me, a bearer – body, arms, emptied.

In the city before here I looked
out on the street to birds, Permit
Holder Only Parking, the Property
For Sale Board, to the tree I planted in leaf
and will leave behind with words

births and headstones –
and this moment – the orange sky
above the *bóthar*, my mother barefoot
with the *bó*. My son playing,
grá mo chroí thú, a mhic.

IV

                I heard in my heart again a low new sound
        that I never used to hear or perhaps didn't understand
in the fall of a missed breath, the leaf's drop to the ground.
                    I heard it as he opened his letter from the DWP
and learned he no longer qualified for PIP – that is, money.
                          Heard it in the woman from the MDT
                              discharging her patient into a poverty
                  of ticked boxes and procedures that set him free
                                          to die alone.

V

Porous as pages not written,
the child approaches sleep
and a mother maps a story,
moon, sky, an owl, a tree,
from somewhere beyond
tyres in rain, the highway.
And waits. And waits.

One day, perhaps,
her story will be forgiven.

Old Woman

My hair is gunpowder.
I take a ring from
the finger of the battlefield.
Hide it in my child's clothing.
The English king has a stench
to rival the fish boats of Bunowen;
the child, grown on granite and grass,
steps aboard. Our men fill the hold,
lower the sails, steady the oars.
My guns are ready.

Notes

BOOK ONE

Title Deed (11): adapted from the text of Deeds to the cottage built by my great-grandfather Pat Connolly for his family on Mason Island (*Oílean Máisean*), Connemara, the ruin of which I now own. The building was part of a post-famine Congested Districts Boards relief scheme.

Specimens (13ff): The introduction to this section is made up of extracts from documents written by Charles R. Browne (BA, MD, MRIA), a 19th-century anthropologist based at Trinity College Dublin. I first read his reports of Mason Island life at Tom Geary's house on the Island. Tom sadly died in 2025 and is greatly missed. The extracts are from Charles R. Browne, *The Ethnography of Inishbofin and Inishark, County Galway,* and from *The Ethnography of Carna and Mweenish, in the Parish of Moyruss, Connemara* (Source: Proceedings of the Royal Irish Academy [1889–1901]).

Blunt Needles (16): For Enid Hooper, an English textile designer who spent many years visiting Mason Island. A short extract from her journal can be seen on page 34. Her collection of writings and drawings from the Carna area are held in the archive of Acadamh na hOllscolaíochta Gaeilge, Carna.

Physiography: 1 & 2 (19 & 23) draws on Charles R. Browne's reports, listings of local surnames and his observations of my ancestors. The list of birds and flora is drawn from my own observations on Mason Island.

Women Come to Find Me (21): *sí*, a 'fairy' magical place

Snow (24): inspired by the photographer Nic Dunlop who left film to develop beneath the battlefield of Aughrim, Co. Galway. His work, with text from Richard Murphy's poem about the battle, was exhibited in *The Battle of Aughrim 1691* at Galway Museum, Ireland in 2025. The poem 'Snow' is also inspired by James Joyce's short story, 'The Dead', from his collection *Dubliners*. *Droim* translates as the ridge or back of a hill.

Na Ceachtanna: Lessons (25) mostly translated within the poems. *Mamó* is an affectionate word for grandmother; Dara Ó Briain and Jonathan Ross are television personalities.

Adúirt mo Mhamó (30) translates as 'my grandmother said' and *beannachtaí* as blessings. **Adúirt mo Mhamó arís** (41): my grandmother said again. The voice of my grandmother is an imagined meeting between her as a child and Charles R. Browne, the anthropologist. His lines when quoted for the second and third times are fictional.

An Ghaeltacht (31): areas in Ireland where Irish is spoken locally.

Place Names (32): this poem uses the familiar place names for territory around Mason Island (*Oileáin Máisean*) and Rusheenamanagh (*Roisín na Mainiach*). Mac Dara is a locally venerated saint who built a chapel in the sixth century on the neighbouring island to Mason which is named for him. *Tadhg Na Buile* was a Connemara chieftain from the O'Flaherty tribe, renowned for his cruelty. He had a castle at Ard East. *Iorras Aithneach* is known as the stormy peninsula for good reason: the wind is a constant. *Cruach na Caoile* is a small island close to Mason Island where deer once grazed.

From the Kitchen on the Edge (35): 'Does the sea hurt' – a phrase inspired by Alice Oswald's line 'And yet again water still in acute discomfort' in her collection *Nobody* (Jonathan Cape, 2019, p. 24).

Back Tonight to a Deserted House (36): *Dia duit*: hello.

Ethnology (44): I campaigned alongside the people of Inishbofin Island and other west-coast community representatives to secure the return and burial of human remains stolen in 1890 from burial grounds in the west of Ireland. The Anatomy Department at Trinity College Dublin acquired the remains in 1892 and displayed them as part of its Anthropological Collection. J.M. Synge referred to the skulls in his play, *Playboy of the Western World*: 'Did you never hear tell of the skulls they have in the city of Dublin, ranged like blue jugs in a cabin of Connaught?' Alfred Cort Hadden and Andrew Francis Dixon stole the Inishbofin remains – thirteen skulls – from St Colman's Monastery during a survey of fishing grounds around the island. They were biologists who became the first generation of academic anthropologists. Charles R. Browne, who is quoted earlier in this book, was a medical doctor/anthropologist who followed Haddon and Dixon to 'Bofin in 1893 and attempted to steal more skulls, but the local people protected the remains of their ancestors and Browne went away empty-handed.

BOOK TWO

Epigraph (45) from J.M.Synge, *The Aran Islands* (Penguin Twentieth Century Classics, 1992, p. 113).

Waters Break (47): *Marias* refers to the saying of the Rosary. *A ghrá mo chroí* was a phrase I heard repeated often in my childhood: love of my heart.

Rough Translation (48): my mother had this dream when I was a child and believed it was a sign of approaching death. The sequence is a conversation between her and me – real and imagined. In part II, the phrase 'They will want you to succeed but never more than them' is taken from Ocean Vuong's *On Earth We're Briefly Gorgeous* (Jonathan Cape, 2019). The phrase 'the squat pen rests' is borrowed from Seamus Heaney's poem 'Digging' from *Death of a Naturalist*.

Straight Lines (53): written in response to Eavan Boland's collection, *The Historians* (Carcanet, 2020). It touches on what I can't own within an Irish poetic legacy and yet what haunts in the blood.

Source (54): an inspiration is Cathal Ó Searcaigh's poem 'An Tobar' ('The Well') and his lines *'Aimsigh do thobar féin, a chroí,/ óir tá am an anáis romhainn amach:/ Caithfear pilleadh arís ar na foinsí'*, translated by Gabriel Fitzmaurice as 'Seek out your own well my dear/ for the age of want is near:/ There will have to be a going back to sources' in *An Bealach 'na Bhaile / Homecoming* (Cló Iar-Chonnachta, 1993).

Caoineadh (56): a lament, a keening for my mother Bríd, whose body is buried in England, and inspired by Eibhlín Dubh Ní Chonaill's classic lament for her husband Airt Ó Laoghaire.

Credo (59): This epigraph is a personal truth and a quest.

BOOK THREE

The epigraph is quoted in my copy of *Love Songs of Connacht* by Douglas Hyde (Irish University Press, Shannon, Ireland, 1968), first edition, *Abhráin Grádh Chúige Connacht* (London and Dublin, 1893). The battered volume is never far from my side. Hyde was a scholar of the Irish language and served as the first President of Ireland. The book is a collection of poems he collected in the West of Ireland, in Irish and English. The sequence that follows, **Mythology** (63), is a conversation with Hyde, creating new poetry and slipping occasionally into re-translation, in the voice of an imagined young Irish woman.

Crow (68) remembers where Ted Hughes wrote much of his collection of the same name, in a house overlooking Cashel Bay.

Body of the Boat (69): the *Ave Maria* is the name of the boat once owned by the poet Richard Murphy and immortalised in his poem, 'The Last Galway Hooker'. Murphy built a business taking tourists and literary celebrities between Cleggan and the island of Inishbofin in north Connemara. The boat is now a wreck in the boatyard of a distant cousin. 'Succursal' is a word from Murphy's poem 'Portico', referring to what he calls his 'deviate church'; the nicknames 'Sex' and 'Lost' are mine for Murphy's close friend Tony White and Murphy himself.

Anraith (70) is dedicated to the exceptional scholar, writer and cartographer Tim Robinson, who chronicled the history, landscape, folklore and place names of Connemara over decades. I met Tim and his wife Máiréad at their flat in London, where they had only recently moved from their home in Roundstone, Connemara, shortly before he died in 2020. I had left my umbrella in their hall and we agreed that I should come and retrieve it, but it was never to be. *Anraith*, soup, refers to the soup kitchen that was built in Moyrus to feed locals, but also tempt them into the Protestant religion, during the famine. Details of the events in this poem can be found in Robinson's *Connemara: A Little Gaelic Kingdom* (Penguin Ireland, 2011, p.149).

Man at Rosroe (72): is the philosopher Ludwig Wittgenstein who lived for a brief period in a bungalow on the harbour at Rosroe in North Connemara in the 1940s. The conversation with his brother can be found in *The Selected Writings of Maurice O'Connor Drury: On Wittgenstein, Philosophy, Religion and Psychiatry*, ed. John Hayes (Bloomsbury, 2017).

At the Michael Hartnett Festival (73) is inspired by the poet who famously switched from writing in English to Irish. His muse in the poem is the poet and singer Caitlín Maude.

Folklore Collector (74) is dedicated to the scholar Rionach Uí Ógáin, former Director of the National Folklore Collection, University College Dublin, and to my friend, Seán Ó Guairim, whose family were neighbours of the Connollys. The references to Marx, Hegel and Ricoeur reflect my befuddled preoccupations with politics and cultural translation. An *óstán* is an hotel, and in this case refers to the Carna Bay Hotel.

The poem **Joe** (77) is for my grandfather, Joe Connolly. The poem recalls a planned meeting between him and the folk collector Séamus Ennis, who refers to this near meeting in *Going to the Well for Water: The Séamus Ennis Field Diary 1942–1946*, ed. Rionach Uí Ógáin (Cork University Press, 2009).

The Singer's Centenary: Carna (78) blends my memory of attending this event, celebrating the life and work of the great *sean-nós* singer Joe Heaney (Seosamh Ó hÉannaí, 1919-94) and a private letter to me from my friend, the poet Glyn Hughes (1935-2011), in which he claimed his former wife had an affair with the singer.

Coventry Carol (80) recalls my childhood in Coventry, England at a time of intense IRA activity.

Playwrights (82) my playful response to the playwrights J.M Synge, Brian Friel and Martin McDonagh who have set their work in Irish cottages.

BOOK FOUR

This section is for my son Connor Robinson (1992-2021) who loved Mason Island.

The epigraph (85) was inspired by Alice Oswald's *Nobody*.

Samhain (88): the month of November in Irish, the month of the dead. The legend of Cailleach and Manannán is described by Manchán Magan (1970-2025) in his book *Thirty-Two Words for Field: Lost Words of the Irish Landscape* (Gill Books, 2020). The word *cailleach* has many meanings, including a bird like a heron or cormorant, a sorceress, an old hag, or a witch.

After (89): Following an autopsy, I buried my son's heart on Mason Island. The Bens refers to the mountains seen from the island. I passed the Welsh Black Mountains on my journey from England to the Irish ferry at Holyhead. A fada is a small right-slanting line over a vowel in Irish and indicates where the letter is pronounced "long". *Cloch na Rón* is the village of Roundstone, on the mainland close to Mason Island. The reference to Dublin 4 is something overheard in south Connemara where locals worry about affluent Dubliners buying up local housing for holiday homes. *Bothár* is a road, *mhic* a son. 'I heard in my heart that low new sound' is inspired by Jamie McKendrick's 'Last Stop Before the Pier Head' in *Poetry Ireland Review*, 139 (2023). DWP: Department for Work and Pensions. PIP: Personal Independence Payment. MDT: Multidisciplinary Team (medical).

Old Woman (97): for the 16th-century noblewoman and dynastic leader, Grace O' Malley (Gráinne Ní Mháille).

ACKNOWLEDGEMENTS

Thanks are due to friends and colleagues holding the Iorras Aithneach peninsula of south Connemara in their hearts: most particularly Seán Ó Guairim, Nic Dunlop, Tom Geary, Máirtín McDonagh, Paddy Mhéime Ó Súilleabháin and Rionach Uí Ógáin. To my colleagues in the Haddon-Dixon Repatriation Project, notably Ciarán Walsh and Marie Coyne. And to the editors of publications in which some of this work, or versions, have appeared: the Melos Press (*Rough Translation*); *Agenda*, *The High Window*, *Poetry London* and *14 Magazine*. I have benefitted from the hugely appreciated support offered by the Heinrich Böll Residency (Achill Island), the Hawthornden Fellowship and an Arts Council England DYCP Award, which allowed me precious time to work with the insightful Pascale Petit.

Thanks also to Paddy Bushe, who cast a clear editor's eye and poetic understanding of the Irish language on the collection, and to my hugely respected Irish teachers, Terri Lynk of the Manchester Irish Language Group and Dr Ian Malcolm. Oh, how you all must have suffered.

Most particularly, I want to thank Maura Dooley, who has been a valued mentor and friend during the course of this work. Also William Palmer, David Morley, Jonathan Taylor and Maureen Freely, who have supported the idea of this book for so long. I have also benefitted from the kind encouragement of Richard Skinner, Jonathan Davidson, Ellen McAteer, Ian Pople, John F. Deane, Stephen Knight, Luke Thompson, John O'Donohue, now sadly gone, and David Constantine. I am grateful to Neil Astley for his faith in publishing this book.

A huge thank you for their comradeship to my friends at the Word Factory, to Garmoe Poets and the North Cornwall Stanza Group.

Grateful thanks and love to the Connolly and Robinson/Galvin families, some of whom are no longer with us. To

Phoebe, Connor, Bryony, Kyra and grandchildren Arabella, Cora, Lotus, Norah May, Radha, Rio and Uma; to my sister Eileen, my mother Bridget and father Patrick, my grandparents Kate and Joe and their other children, Cole, Mícheál, Mary, Sally, Kathleen and Sheila. To the Connollys who supported my ownership of the cottage on Mason Island. To friends Ann Doherty, Jules Smith and Val Curtis. And a special thank you to my husband and island companion, Richard Sharland, whose watercolour of the harbour at Mason Island appears on the cover.

To all of the living, dead and unborn who fill these pages.

ILLUSTRATIONS

FRONTISPIECE: South Connemara section of Tim Robinson's *Folding Landscapes* map of Connemara reproduced with kind permission of the Royal Irish Academy and with huge thanks to Professor John Drever and Aifric Downey, Aisling Keane and Nessa Cronin.

13: Anthropometry (measuring skulls) on Inishbofin, 1892 or 1893, from the collection of Dr Charles R. Browne (186[7]–1918), consisting of six albums of images from the western islands as well as scenes of Dublin and Trinity College (ref. MS10961-1_32). This photograph and the others on pages 62 and 67 are reproduced by kind permission of the Board of Trinity College Dublin.

46: Grandparents Kate and Joe Connolly with mother Bridget (Bríd Ní Chonghaile).

62: Photographs taken in the Aran Islands from another of Charles R. Browne's albums (ref. MS10961-4_07).

86: Connor Robinson (1992-2021), photo by Nic Dunlop.

COVER PAINTING: *From the Quay on Mason Island* (2022) by Richard Sharland.

Cathy Galvin's first full-length book of poetry, *Ethnology: a love song for Connemara* (Bloodaxe Books, 2026) follows three pamphlet sequences, *Black & Blue* (Melos Press, 2014), *Rough Translation* (Melos Press, 2016) and *Walking the Coventry Ring Road with Lady Godiva* (Guillemot Press, 2019). She has been shortlisted for several awards including the Ilkley Poetry Prize and Listowel Poetry Prize, and is the recipient of a Hawthornden Fellowship, Heinrich Böll (Achill Island) residency and an Arts Council England DYCP award. Her work has appeared in publications including *Agenda*, *14 Magazine*, *The High Window*, *The London Magazine*, *Morning Star* and *Poetry London*.

As a journalist, she has worked on staff as a senior editor for *Newsweek* and *The Sunday Times* and is a non-executive director of *The Tablet*. She was the editor of *Red*, an anthology of new writing published by Waterstones.

As well as a poet and journalist, she has been a champion of other writers and writing, co-founding the *Sunday Times* EFG Short Story Award and founding and directing The Word Factory short story organisation.

With roots in Coventry and Connemara, she now lives near Bodmin Moor in Cornwall.

EU DECLARATION OF GPSR CONFORMITY

Books published by Bloodaxe Books are identified by the EAN/ISBN printed above our address on the copyright page and manufactured by the printer whose address is noted below. This declaration of conformity is issued under the sole responsibility of the publisher, the object of declaration being each individual book produced in conformity with the relevant EU harmonisation legislation with no known hazards or warnings, and is made on behalf of Bloodaxe Books Ltd on 26 February 2026 by Neil Astley, Managing Director, editor@bloodaxebooks.com.

No part of this book may be used or reproduced in any manner for the purpose of training artificial intelligence technologies or systems. The publisher expressly reserves *Ethnology: a love poem for Connemara* from the text and data mining exception in accordance with European Parliament Directive (EU) 2019/790.